CLARINETS

by Pamela K. Harris

MIDLOTHIAN PUBLIC LIBRARY
14701 S. KENTON AVENUE
MIDLOTHIAN, IL 60445

Published by The Child's World®
1980 Lookout Drive • Mankato, MN 56003-1705
800-599-READ • www.childsworld.com

Design element: Vector memory/Shutterstock.com
Photo credits: 123RF: 18; Alenavlad/Shutterstock.com: 21 (oboe); Andrea Nissotti/Shutterstock.
com: 21 (flute); Andriy Dovzhykov/123RF: 15; Andrey_Popov/Shutterstock.com: 12; Boris Medvedev/
Shutterstock.com: 21 (piccolo); daisydaisy/123RF: 11; Emanuele Ravecca/Shutterstock.com: cover, 1;
furtseff/Shutterstock.com: 18, 21 (bassoon); horiyan/Shutterstock.com: 21 (saxophone); KatyKing27/
Shutterstock.com: 8; Mariia Mykhaliuk/Shutterstock.com: 16; Matthias G. Ziegler/Shutterstock.
com: 7; Rey Borlaza/Shutterstock.com: 4; Wilawan Khasawong/123RF: 21 (recorder)

ISBN: 9781503831896
LCCN: 2018960413

Printed in the United States of America
PA02417

Table *of* Contents

CHAPTER ONE

The Clarinet

The band marches by playing a happy tune. A whole row of the band is playing what look like long, black sticks. The sticks make a special, mellow sound. What instrument are they playing? Why, the clarinet, of course!

Clarinets belong to a group of instruments called **woodwinds**. Woodwinds are tubed-shaped instruments that make sounds when you blow air through them. To make different sounds, you cover up the holes on the instrument. Saxophones and flutes are woodwinds, too.

❮ *Marching bands often have lots of clarinets.*

CHAPTER TWO

Different Kinds of Clarinets

The first clarinets were made from wood. Now they are made from metal, plastic, and even glass! Clarinets also come in different sizes. The smallest kind

The most common type of clarinet is called the B-flat clarinet.

of clarinet is the **soprano clarinet**. The biggest clarinet is the **bass clarinet**. The bass clarinet is so big, some players must put one end on the ground to play it!

Bass clarinets like this one are about 40 inches (102 cm) tall. ❯

CHAPTER THREE

The Mouthpiece

To play a woodwind instrument, you must blow air through the **mouthpiece**. A clarinet mouthpiece has a flat, thin piece of **reed** attached by a metal band. The reed covers a hole at the top of the clarinet. When you blow on the mouthpiece, the reed opens and closes the hole very fast. This makes the air inside the clarinet **vibrate**, or move back and forth. The moving air makes the sound that you hear.

❮ *The clarinet's reed works best if it is kept wet. You keep the reed wet by licking it.*

CHAPTER FOUR

The Air

Have you ever made a whistle from a blade of grass? Try it and see what happens. Press a wide blade of grass between your thumbs. Close your lips almost all the way and blow hard on the grass. Can you make a sound?

A person who plays a clarinet is called a clarinetist.

The sound from the blade of grass is much like the sound from a clarinet. As you blow over the grass, you make it vibrate. As you blow over the reed on a clarinet, you make it vibrate, too.

Anyone can play the clarinet. ❯

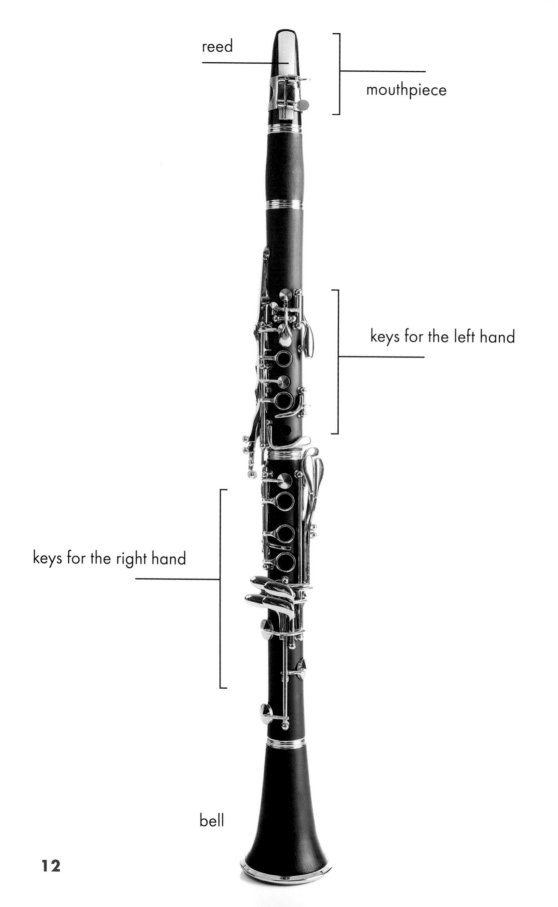

reed

mouthpiece

keys for the left hand

keys for the right hand

bell

CHAPTER FIVE

The Shape

The body of a clarinet is shaped like a long tube. The length of the tube changes the way the clarinet sounds. Shorter tubes make higher sounds, or **notes**. Longer tubes make lower notes. To make different notes, the clarinet has many holes. Covering lots of holes with your fingers makes the clarinet play low notes. Leaving lots of holes open makes the clarinet play high notes.

Many people believe that a German man named Johann Denner invented the clarinet around 1700.

CHAPTER SIX

The Keys

Clarinets have almost 20 holes. You can reach some of the holes easily with your fingers. Others are harder to reach. **Keys** help you reach all of the holes. The keys are really buttons with pads attached to them. Certain pads cover some of the clarinet's holes. Other pads sit above the holes, but leave them open. By pressing the keys, you move the pads on and off the holes. Then you can make different notes.

The keys help cover some of the holes on the clarinet. ❯

CHAPTER SEVEN

Playing the Clarinet

To play a clarinet, you must move your fingers quickly to cover different holes. You also need to blow hard and not let any air escape. The muscles in your face become very strong when you play the clarinet!

Clarinets are popular in jazz and classical music.

❮ *Clarinet players hold the instrument out from their body.*

CHAPTER EIGHT

Sounds of the Clarinet

Clarinets can make all kinds of sounds. Some sounds the clarinet makes are like a whisper or a growl. Other sounds are like ducks quacking or a person singing. Clarinets can sound happy or sad. They can also make the loudest sounds of the woodwind instruments!

Some famous clarinet players include Benny Goodman, Sabine Meyer, and Woody Herman.

❮ *This girl can make many sounds with her clarinet.*

People play clarinets to make many kinds of music. Clarinets are popular in jazz music and in music from many parts of the world. Clarinets are also used to play classical music. Would you like to play the clarinet?

Other Woodwind Instruments

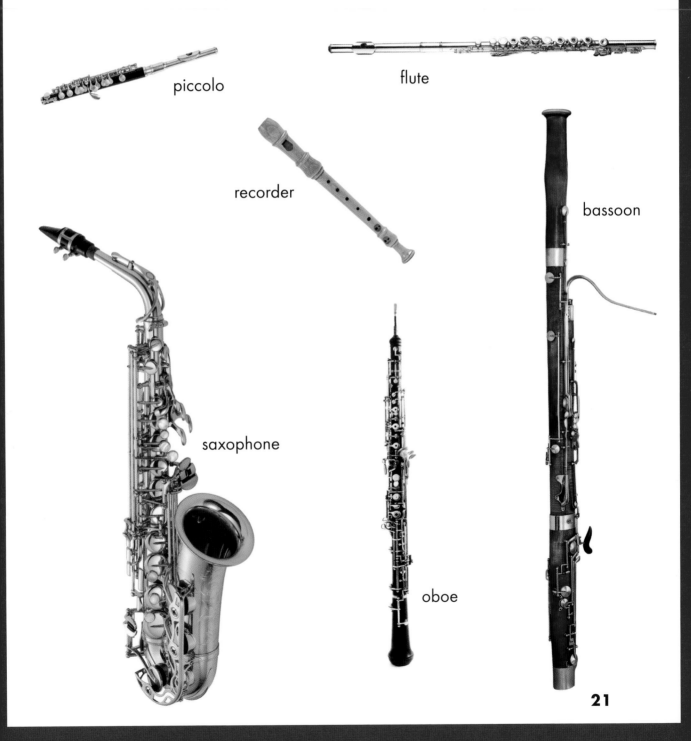

piccolo

flute

recorder

bassoon

saxophone

oboe

Glossary

bass clarinet (BAYSS klayr-ih-NET) A bass clarinet is a very big clarinet. It plays very low notes.

keys (KEEZ) The keys of a clarinet are the buttons that help cover the clarinet's holes. The clarinet has many keys.

moutpiece (MOWTH-peese) The mouthpiece of a clarinet is where you put your mouth to play it. Blowing air through the mouthpiece creates sounds.

notes (NOHTS) A note is a musical sound. By pressing different keys on a clarinet, a player can make different notes.

reed (REED) A reed is a type of tall grass. A thin piece of reed is used in the mouthpiece of a clarinet to make sounds.

soprano clarinet (suh-PRA-noh klayr-ih-NET) A soprano clarinet is the smallest type of common clarinet. It can play very high notes.

vibrate (VY-brayt) When something vibrates, it moves back and forth. When air vibrates inside of a clarinet, it makes a sound.

woodwinds (WOOD-windz) Woodwinds are tube-shaped instruments that are played by blowing air into a mouthpiece. Clarinets are woodwinds.

To Learn More

IN THE LIBRARY

Landau, Elaine. *Is the Clarinet for You?* Minneapolis, MN: Lerner Publications, 2014.

Nunn, Daniel. *Woodwind.* Chicago, IL: Heinemann Library, 2012.

Sloan, Carolyn. *Welcome to the Symphony: A Musical Exploration of the Orchestra Using Beethoven's Symphony No. 5.* New York, NY: Workman Publishing, 2015.

ON THE WEB

Visit our website for links about clarinets:

childsworld.com/links

Note to Parents, Teachers, and Librarians: We routinely verify our Web links to make sure they are safe and active sites. So encourage your readers to check them out!

Index

About the Author

Pamela K. Harris grew up in Oregon and currently lives in Denver, Colorado. She directs a non-profit organization that provides early childhood education to children from low-income backgrounds. She has testified before Congress on the importance of early childhood education. She loves being a student herself and has a PhD in Educational Leadership.